Your friendship means the world to me

pictures and verse
by
Sandra Magsamen

gift

stewart tabori & chang

You
are kind,
thoughtful
and gentle
too.

I
love the
time I
spend with
you.

Hanging
out is
always fun.

Happily we've let few adventures go undone.

Some escapades have been a thrill...

We've learned about ourselves when we sat still.

We've cried
until we
laughed

and laughed
until
we cried.

There is
nothing in our
lives we
would not
confide.

I'm your honesty I have come to depend...

Thank you
for being
my
friend.

You have been
by my side
through ups
and downs,

thick

and

thin.

Caring
and loyalty
you give
without
question.

You
are family,
like a sister.
You
are kin.

Published in 2001 by
Stewart, Tabori & Chang
A division of Harry N. Abrams, Inc.
115 West 18th Street
New York, NY 10011

Distributed in Canada by
General Publishing Company Ltd.
30 Lesmill Road
Don Mills, Ontario, Canada M3B2J6

ISBN: 1-58479-067-9

Printed in Hong Kong

10 9 8 7 6 5 4 3 2 1

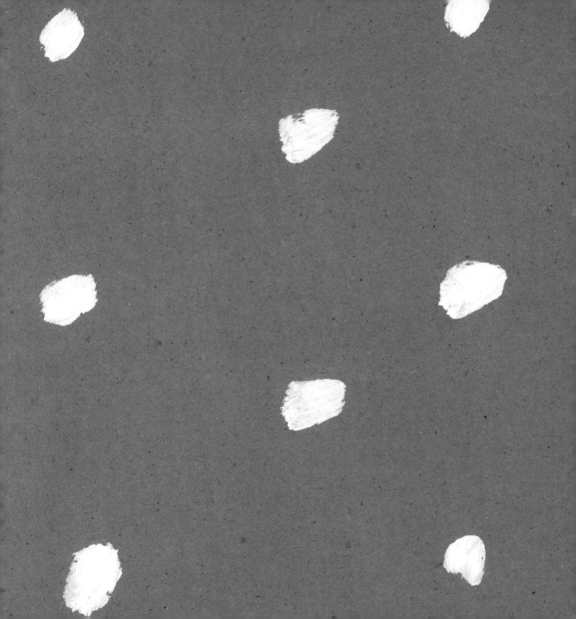